Exploring

The

Bible

and How to Study It

Karen Rizzi

978-1-0687264-0-8

Published by Yours Faithfully Limited
www.yours-faithfully.co.uk

DEDICATION

To my grandchildren

Taylor, Esmé and Poppy.

Contents

Foundations of Faith Series

This series of books is your companion for stepping into the world of Christianity. Whether you have decided to follow Christ or are simply curious about what it means to live a Christian life, these books are written just for you.

Starting on a new spiritual path can be both exciting and daunting. Some people liken it to walking through the wardrobe into the land of Narnia as the children did in "The Lion, the Witch and the Wardrobe" (C. S. Lewis). Others will relate to stepping out of the Tardis into an unknown time and place (Dr. Who).

"A Guide for New Christians" is designed to help you take your first steps in faith. Inside, you discover straightforward explanations of core beliefs, practical insights, and encouraging words. These help deepen your understanding and enrich your relationship with God.

Whether you come from a background of no faith or are seeking to rediscover your spiritual roots, these books equip you with the knowledge and tools you need to thrive in your Christian life.

Join the countless others who have transformed their lives through faith. It is time to deepen your understanding of God and embrace the incredible life ahead.

Your journey starts here.

Introduction

A Guide to the Bible

What comes to mind when you think "Bible"? After all, it is a book, and I doubt that you will ever pick up one and say to yourself, "This is a new thing for me. Does it have a user guide?" As long as it is written in a language you can read, it is like most other books.

You read a fiction book from beginning to end. It starts with an introduction to the plot and people, moves through the storyline and ends with a revelation or a conclusion. Think "Once upon a time.....", this happened, that happened, finishing with "they all lived happily ever after."

A non-fiction book informs you about a particular topic. As you read it, it reveals facts, working from basic principles through more complicated stages. In a mathematics book, it would not make sense to read about algebra before learning addition and subtraction. Of course, the author should make clear their assumptions about the level of skill you require before you start reading the book.

Finally, there's the anthology, a series of articles written by different authors around a central theme. When reading this type of book, you can pick which chapters to read and in what order.

What type of book is the Bible? It is non-fiction, but when trying to read it from beginning to end, most people do not get very far before giving up. Is anthology a better fit? The Bible is, indeed, a series of articles by different authors around the central topic of God's love and his relationship with people. Dipping in and choosing what to read does not satisfy either. At any point, what you are reading relates to something written about earlier in the Bible and also points towards something you will read later on.

The Bible does not follow the standard instructions for reading a book. It is as though the "handbook for our Christian life" needs its own handbook. This book aims to create a user guide specifically for the Bible so that you can read it with understanding and benefit from all it has to reveal.

What is the Bible?

The Bible is the backbone of Christian life. It is the written handbook God has given us. Without this book, we would be lost. It underpins our lives as Christians, so we must value it, trust it and know how to navigate it. Let us demystify the Bible in this book so that when we see it quoted elsewhere, we will be able to follow along with confidence.

The Bible is also called:
- The Scriptures.
- The Holy Scriptures.
- The Word of God.

In this book, we use "The Bible".

The Bible says of itself:

> The law of the Lord is "sweeter also than honey." Psalm 19:10.

> "Your word is a lamp to my feet and a light to my path." Psalm 119:105.

> "Is not my word like fire, declares the Lord, and like a hammer that breaks the rock in pieces?" Jeremiah 23:29.

> "For the word of God is living and active, sharper than any two-edged sword, piercing to the division of soul and of spirit, of joints and of marrow, and discerning the thoughts and intentions of the heart." Hebrews 4:12.

> "All Scripture is breathed out by God and profitable for teaching, for reproof, for correction, and for training in righteousness, that the man of God may be complete, equipped for every good work." 2 Timothy 3:16-17.

The Message of the Bible

Its essence. What it tells us.

The Bible centres around the one and only God, the creator of all that exists. It documents his relationship with people, showing his will and purpose as a just, loving, and ultimately prevailing God.

The first portion of the Bible documents the history of the world from creation to the Israelite's exile in Babylon in the fourth century BC. It covers their life, their search for the Promised Land and what happened once they had arrived there. God always wanted a relationship with the Israelites, but they were not always faithful in following his ways, preferring to be independent of him. God gave them many chances to return to him, sending prophets with his condemnations and encouragements. Sometimes, the people turned their lives around, only to fail again.

The second portion of the Bible begins by telling of the life, death and resurrection of Jesus Christ. He fulfilled the sacrificial laws God set down for the Israelites. In so doing, an individual no longer has to make a sacrifice to atone for each of their wrong-doings. The death of Jesus is the only sacrifice required, allowing anyone who believes in his death and resurrection to be reconciled to God.

The Bible is God's "Love Story"

The Bible finishes by documenting the lives of the early believers as they work out how to live as followers of Christ.

The Bible is more than a history book; its content applies to each generation that reads it. It contains some thought-provoking philosophy, though it does not argue for or against the existence of God. This discussion was not needed, as all the authors knew him personally.

The Bible has much general value, too. Many of the laws given to the Israelites benefitted their health and provided a system of justice that is still in use today.

The Bible is foundational to the Christian faith. It shows how God reveals himself to every person. He continually looks after each one, pursuing them even when they disobey him and get into trouble. God is always willing to forgive them and us. He offers the promise of salvation through Jesus Christ and calls for people to live according to God's will. Overall, the message of the Bible encourages everyone to have a personal relationship with God, to love one another, and to seek His guidance in all aspects of life. In essence, it is God's "Love Story".

For an understanding of salvation, see This is Salvation in Appendix G.

The History of the Bible

How the Bible became what it is today

The first books of the Bible were written in Hebrew as early as the tenth century BC. In the eighth century BC, the royal scribes began recording the history of the kings and their heroic deeds. The Israelites were careful to ensure that they faithfully recorded what God said and did. By the sixth century BC, the Pentateuch (the first five books of the Bible) was "canonised", i.e. fixed in content and presented order. By the first century BC, scholars had established the books that make up the Hebrew scriptures. For more information, see Old Testament Timeline in Appendix B.

These are the scriptures that Jesus knew well and quoted from. However, the order of the books differed significantly from what we see today.

The third and second centuries BC saw the Hebrew scriptures translated into Greek, a dominant language of the Roman Empire. King Ptolemy of Egypt commissioned this, gathering together 72 men, six from each of the tribes of Israel. They worked in separate rooms, translating the Pentateuch into Greek. Documents from the time report that all 72 translations were identical. We know this version as the Septuagint, named after the Greek for seventy. King Ptolemy deposited a copy in the library in Alexandria. The Septuagint was later extended to include a Greek translation of the whole of the Hebrew scriptures.

Extra books, only existing in Greek, document the history of Israel from the third to first centuries BC. These books collectively make up the Apocrypha. Roman Catholic and Greek Orthodox Bibles include this section. The Protestant church never approved the Apocrypha and did not add it to their Bible.

The remaining books, written in Greek in the first century AD, document Jesus' life and the establishment of the Christian church.

For more information on these Greek books, see New Testament Timeline in Appendix C.

The earliest known manuscript of the Bible is the fourth-century Codex Sinaiticus. In the 19th century, archaeologists found several hundred of its pages in St Catherine's monastery on Mount Sinai. The collection includes the Septuagint, half of the Hebrew Old Testament, and a complete New Testament from the fourth century. Digitised copies of these pages are online at codexsinaiticus.org, with most of the originals housed in the British Museum.

In AD 405, Pope Damasus I authorised a Latin translation of the Bible. This is known as the Latin Vulgate.

In the fifth century, the churches canonised the content of the New Testament. At the same time, they renamed the previously agreed-upon Hebrew scriptures the "Old Testament".

> The Bible's content was fixed in 5th century.

In the eighth century, Bede, a monk and scholar, created the first English translation when he translated the Gospel of John.

In the 14th century, John Wycliffe, a Catholic priest and theologian, played a crucial role in creating the first complete translation of the Bible into English. This was before the invention of the printing press, with each copy taking about ten months to produce. Amazingly, one hundred and seventy copies of the Wycliffe Bible survive today. This made the

Bible available to those who did not understand Latin. As a consequence, the Catholic church ostracised Wycliffe for undermining its power and control of the people.

The following century saw William Tyndale, an English priest, produce an English translation of the Bible directly from the Hebrew and Greek texts.

In the 16th century, the Dutch scholar Desiderius Erasmus compiled a Greek copy of the New Testament based on a few late medieval manuscripts. Several other scholars later refined and edited this version, known as the Textus Receptus.

In 1611, King James I of England commissioned a new English translation. This version, the King James Version (KJV), drew heavily from Tyndale's translation and the Textus Receptus. It remained unaltered for 250 years and was the standard text used at church services. It influenced the English language with many of its phrases familiar to the general population even today, for example:

"A man after his own heart." 1 Samuel 13:14.

The writing is on the wall – a paraphrase of Danel 5:5-6.

Spare the rod, spoil the child – a summary of Proverbs 13:24.

"There is nothing new under the sun." Ecclesiastes 1:9.

"There is no peace," says the Lord, "for the wicked." Isaiah 48:22.

"For the love of money is a root of all kinds of evils." 1 Timothy 6:10.

More recently, modern scholars and translators use newer critical editions of the Greek New Testament rather than the Textus Receptus. There is an ongoing debate about which source is more accurate.

Today, the Bible has been translated into many languages in various styles. See What Bible Translations are Available on page 29.

It is not true to say that the current Bibles are one translation on top of another. Those available today are retranslations of the original manuscripts, not ones translated from Greek into Latin, Latin into Old English, and Old English into our familiar English language.

English Bibles are translated from the original Hebrew or Greek versions.

The Structure of the Bible

At least 40 authors from all walks of life, including shepherds, kings, doctors, and fishermen, wrote the 66 discrete books that make up the Bible.

The Bible has two sections: the Old Testament and the New Testament. Both testaments present their books in a thematic order rather than in the order in which the events occurred.

The Old Testament

The Old Testament starts with the 'History' books, Genesis to Esther. These books tell of the relationship between God and his people, beginning with Adam and Eve and their disobedience towards him. Next are accounts that you may be familiar with: Noah's Ark, Abraham and Isaac, Moses and the exodus from Egypt, and the succession of kings of Israel and Judah who either followed the teachings of God or blatantly disobeyed them.

Scholars have corroborated much of the Bible's historical content.

These books show a loving God encouraging his people to leave their wicked ways behind and return to his blessing. Sometimes, they did return, but God did not give up on his people even when they chose not to.

This 'history' section is easy to read. It alternates between the good times under God's hand and the difficult times when the people's disobedience resulted in sickness, violence, unrest and death.

Contemporary historians and, more recently, archaeologists have corroborated much of this historical content.

The next section of the Old Testament falls under the category of 'Poetry and Wisdom'. These books, from Job to the Song of Solomon, are full of highs and lows: prayers and praises, love and joy through to despair, doubts and anger. They cover everything from triumphant faith when people include God in daily life to the emptiness experienced when living without God.

Many find the books of Psalms and Proverbs helpful when navigating life's ups and downs.

The final section of the Old Testament comprises the books from Isaiah to Malachi. These are full of prophecies, arranged in order of the prophets' seniority, from the major ones, for example, Isaiah and Jeremiah, to the minor ones, including Amos and Micah. These books contain God's words to his people. They warn of the judgement and consequential doom that will come upon the people if they choose to live as though God docs not matter. On the positive side, these prophecies also proclaim the coming of a Messiah, who will suffer the judgment meant for man, thereby offering a new relationship with God.

Whenever Jesus quoted from the scripture, he was referring to the Old Testament.

Both the Christian and Jewish communities regard the Old Testament as holy writings. The Jewish version has the books in a different order with their own chapter and verse divisions. As the Jews are still waiting for the coming of the Messiah, their scriptures end there.

The New Testament

The New Testament follows the life of Christ. It explains what Christ's death accomplished and how we can partake of the new life that this offers.

Jesus often referred to the Old Testament by saying, "It is written",

Its first section, from Matthew to John, is the 'Gospels' or 'Good News', covering the life of Christ whilst he was here on earth. These four books are each written from a different perspective, giving an all-round view of Christ.

Then follows the 'Acts of the Apostles', again written by Luke. It covers the life of the disciples after Christ left this earth and documents the establishment of the church. Much like the Old Testament, contemporary writers, especially Josephus, a 1st-century Romano-Jewish historian, have corroborated the events in the Gospels and Acts.

The remaining books are letters (or epistles) written by the early Christian leaders to the churches they had established on their travels. Though specific churches received these letters, they were copied and passed around the local congregations. These letters unpack what it means to follow Christ and live a Christian life.

The last book is "Revelations of John", a prophecy given in a dream to John, the gospel writer. It is traditionally accepted that this book records a vision of the end times and encourages the church to 'get itself in order'. Some of the imagery appears complicated or obscure. If it seems difficult to understand, the main thing to remember is that it talks about the future when Satan is finally defeated and God wins.

This concludes the Bible that you will find in most Christian churches. As noted in the previous chapter, "The History of the Bible", the Roman Catholic and Greek Orthodox Bibles include The Apocrypha. It is either an extra section between the Old and New Testaments or spread throughout the Old Testament.

Reference markers have been added to make sharing the Bible with others easy. Each book is divided into chapters and further subdivided into verses, annotated in numerical order. Scholars added these divisions to the original Old Testament in the 13th century and to the New Testament texts in the 16th century.

The standard format for quoting a section of the Bible is Book Chapter Verse. When referencing the first verse of the first chapter of the Gospel of John, you would say, "John chapter 1 verse 1", often shortened to "John 1:1".

Book names are often abbreviated. For the standard abbreviations and where to find each book in the Bible, see Book Name Abbreviations in Appendix A.

History in the Bible

The thread that holds it together.

In the beginning, there was Genesis, an account of the creation of the universe. God gave the Earth's first inhabitants, Adam and Eve, his instructions for living on the Earth - work hard, look after the animals and have me as your God. Adam and Eve decided they could be independent from God. This disobedience, known as "The Fall", led to disharmony, pain and toil coming into their lives, resulting in an estrangement from God.

Their descendants were a mix of God-fearing and God-hating people, the latter being by far the larger group, who had no reverence for nor fear of God. God decided to judge the world. He instructed Noah to build a giant boat ark to rescue his family and many animals from a worldwide flood. Afterwards, God created a rainbow to represent his covenant of faithfulness to his people, promising never to send another flood that would destroy all life.

It was not long before Noah's descendants had, once again, decided to follow their own ways. The faithful few, notably Abraham and his descendants, were blessed by God. God promised Abraham that his descendants would be numbered like the grains of sand. These people became the Hebrew nation, later called Israel after Abraham's grandson.

Following a famine, the first Israelites found themselves enslaved and oppressed in Egypt. God called Moses to lead his people out of Egypt and into the Promised Land (the Exodus). It is clear that Moses knew this God as Yahweh or Jehovah, not a local god but the creator of heaven and earth.

God performed many miracles during this Exodus: he provided food to eat - manna and honey; he guided them with a cloud by day and a fire by night; he parted the Red Sea so that the people could cross safely; he gave them the 10 Commandments. God had personal conversations with Moses. Many of the things he instructed Moses to do point forward to the symbolism of Christ.

As in the beginning, despite experiencing God looking after them, the people rebelled against God and their leaders. Many of the Israelites wanted to go back to Egypt. Their grumbling meant that God kept them 40 years in the desert, so the 'moaning generation' never entered the Promised Land. Those who eventually arrived called the land "Israel". Its future included years of blessing under David and Solomon.

After the death of Solomon, the tribes of Judah and Benjamin broke away from Israel to form Judah. On the whole, Judah stayed more faithful to God than Israel. Eventually, the Babylonians and the Assyrians overran both lands, and God's people entered years characterised by desperation.

> God remained faithful to his people despite their behaviour.

Throughout these times, God remained faithful to his people even though they disobeyed and rejected him. He sent prophets who preached and wrote lengthy condemnations of their behaviour and their lack of faith. The prophets also brought exaltations to change their ways, turn their lives around and stop allying themselves with their enemies.

These prophecies gave the faithful hope that a new leader, the Messiah, in the style of Moses or Elijah, would come to the rescue and redeem God's people once and for all. Of all the prophecies in the Old Testament, there are more than 300 that point towards the coming Messiah. The Gospel writers refer to them in their writings, where they document the fulfilment of these prophecies. (See Prophecies about The Messiah in Appendix E for some examples.)

> Every Gospel is a biography of Christ.

In the New Testament, 400 years after the writing of the last Old Testament book, the Gospels document four accounts of the life of Christ. Their authors were people who found themselves close to the action:

- Matthew – one of the twelve disciples.
- Mark – a personal assistant to Barnabus, Paul and Peter when they visited the new churches.
- Luke – a doctor and historian who travelled with Paul.
- John – a cousin of Jesus, who was part of the inner circle and wrote up his account as an old man.

The gospels complement each other. They are like four images of the same object taken from different angles. Each one describes the object, but the pictures don't look the same. Every gospel is a biography of Christ, documenting his teaching and miracles, finishing with his death and resurrection. This was the culmination of God's plan to rescue mankind from its sin, to allow them to reconcile with God. It did away with the daily sacrifices for sin and replaced it with the one sacrifice of the sinless Son of God. Those who accept this sacrifice as their own become holy and acceptable to God and can enter into his presence.

The book of the Acts of the Apostles follows the lives of the disciples and their efforts to spread the gospel throughout the area, from Italy in the west to Turkey in the east. There's a pivotal moment in Acts chapter 2 when the Holy Spirit, promised by God in John chapter 18, comes upon the disciples, giving them the power to do what Christ did in his life. The focus of this book is on Peter, 'the rock on which I will build my church'. He was later joined by Paul, who, as

Saul, had previously persecuted Christ's followers before his conversion on the road to Damascus.

The remainder of the Bible consists of letters written to churches and named individuals. These were primarily written by Paul and still provide a blueprint for the followers of Christ. The writers both praise and discipline their readers and give the answers to many doctrinal and ethical questions.

Congregations heard these letters read aloud alongside the oral history of Christ's life. These letters were further copied by dedicated scribes and collected into books for distribution across Asia Minor.

The final New Testament writing, the Revelation of John, is a prophecy yet to be fulfilled. It concerns the return of Christ to the Earth to claim all those who have put their faith in him.

A word on the Bible's timeline

The Old Testament can be confusing to read. Its order - history, poetry and then prophecy - does not conform to a timeline from creation to the Exile of the Jews in the fourth century BC.

Listing the Old and New Testament books chronologically enables us to read the poetry and prophecy with greater understanding. And, yes, we need to be reading the Old Testament as it helps to explain much of the symbolism in the New Testament. When Paul wrote in 2 Timothy 3:16, "All Scripture is God-breathed" he was talking about the Old Testament, the only scripture available at the time of writing.

See Old Testament Timeline and New Testament Timeline in the appendices.

Can I Trust the Bible?

We know that the Bible is a collection of books written by many God-believing authors over a long period. Christians believe God inspired all of these writings.

The question for each of us is, "How can I trust what I am reading?" In this chapter, we will explore ways in which we can be assured that the Bible is trustworthy.

The actual words are verified by ancient texts

As we saw in "The History of the Bible" researchers have found many ancient manuscripts that support the Bible's later copies. In fact, it has more supporting documents than most other ancient texts. Of the New Testament. F. F. Bruce, a leading 20th-century biblical scholar, commented,

> "The evidence for our New Testament writings is ever so much greater than the evidence for many writings of classical authors, the authenticity of which no one dreams of questioning. And if the New Testament were a collection of secular writings, their authenticity would generally be regarded as beyond all doubt." The New Testament Documents: Are They Reliable? (1943)

Scientists analysing these texts have shown that there is a remarkable consistency between the versions. Although they found some minor variations, these do not affect any of the significant doctrinal teachings. With the original Hebrew and Greek writings authenticated, it remains that we need to trust the translation we read in our own language. Most Bibles contain an introduction outlining their source text and the method of its translation. There are a plethora of versions today. At one end of the scale are literal translations, and at the other, entirely paraphrased translations. (see What Bible Translations are Available on page 29).

People and places in the Bible can be verified

Many archaeological discoveries underpin the content of the Bible, confirming its historical accuracy. Also, ancient historians and writers, such as Josephus and Pliny the Younger, have independently referred to events, people and places mentioned in the Bible.

Researchers have found several cities once thought fabled, showing that they align with the biblical narrative, e.g. Jericho, Nineveh, and Babylon. Indeed, they continue to discover many things that turn so-called myths into fact. For example:

- In the book of Daniel, chapter 5, a king named Belshazzar sees handwriting on a wall. He asks Daniel to interpret it. For centuries, historians have denied the existence of Belshazzar. The available Babylonian records indicated Nabonitis was the last king of Babylon. Then archaeologists found a clay tablet that revealed the truth: Nabonitis was the father of Belshazzar, and they were co-regents ruling together. Nabonitis travelled the world while his son ruled the kingdom.

  Now, "the third ruler in the kingdom" in Daniel 5:16 is better understood:

  > "But I have heard that you can give interpretations and solve problems. Now if you can read the writing and make known to me its interpretation, you shall be clothed with purple and have a chain of gold around your neck and shall be the third ruler in the kingdom."

- As another example, the Bible states that Moses wrote the books from Genesis to Deuteronomy. People believed that he could not have done so as there was no written language recorded in his time. In 1887, archaeologists found 300 clay tablets in Egypt, at Tel-El-Armana. These were letters and business transactions between Egypt and Palestine dated centuries before Moses was born. This confirms that as well as having a written language, they had a postal service. While these tablets do not prove that Moses himself did the writing, they allow for him or one of his servants to have written them at the time.

As an aside, how did Moses and the Israelites read the Ten Commandments if there was no system of reading and writing?

> "The tablets were the work of God, and the writing was the writing of God, engraved on the tablets." Exodus 32:16.

What if no one had ever found the Egyptian tablets or the Belshazzar tablet? What other things in the Bible will researchers prove in the future? We are called to believe the Bible, although there will be times when our studies of it may be incomplete.

Nelson Glueck, a renowned 20th-century archaeologist and rabbi, wrote,

> "It may be stated categorically that no archaeological discovery has ever controverted a Biblical reference. Scores of archaeological findings have been made which confirm in clear outline or exact detail historical statements in the Bible. And, by the same token, proper evaluation of Biblical descriptions has often led to amazing discoveries" from "Rivers in the Desert" (1959)

Of the New Testament. William F. Albright, another 20th-century leading biblical archaeologist, commented,

> "We can already say emphatically that there is no longer any solid basis for dating any book of the New Testament after about AD 80." From "Toward a More Conservative View." (1963).

Some scholars might disagree with the date but would certainly uphold a date of AD 100. With this in mind, we can see that the New Testament authors were writing when Jesus' principal opponents were still alive. These naysayers would have contradicted anything they believed to be untrue, yet there is a lack of evidence for this.

It is worth noting here that Jesus used many quotes from the established scriptures (the Old Testament). Though the scribes and Pharisees usually disagreed with Jesus' interpretation, they did not contradict the content he used.

Sceptics changing their minds

Some researchers, who initially sought to disprove the Bible, have ended up being convinced of its accuracy. Sir William Ramsay initially agreed with his fellow researchers about Luke's object in writing the Acts of the Apostles.

> Luke's object ".....was not to present a trustworthy picture of facts in the period about A.D. 50, but to produce a certain effect on his own time by setting forth a carefully coloured account of events and persons of that older period. He wrote for his contemporaries, not for truth." from "The Bearing of Recent Discovery on the Trustworthiness of the New Testament" (1914)

Having visited the Middle East to back up his thoughts, he returned, describing Luke's history as:

> "unsurpassed in respect of its trustworthiness" again from "The Bearing of Recent Discovery on the Trustworthiness of the New Testament" (1914)

Another example would be Frank Morison. In his book, "Who Moved the Stone?" (1930), he explores the death and resurrection of Jesus, hoping to show that Jesus' resurrection was a myth. The book follows his thinking, starting as a sceptic and finishing as a believer.

Scientific facts found in the Bible

God gave the Israelites rules and regulations to follow. Scientists have only recently acknowledged that many of these verses describe scientific laws. These include:

- God decreed that a baby boy undergo circumcision on day 8. Scientists have discovered that the agents that form blood clots are at their best on this day:
    - Vitamin K does not reach a sufficient quantity until day 7.
    - Prothrombin is at its highest-ever level (110% of normal) on day 8.

  "And on the eighth day the flesh of his foreskin shall be circumcised." Leviticus 12:3.

- Quarantining helps stop the spread of certain diseases.

  "He shall remain unclean as long as he has the disease. He is unclean. He shall live alone. His dwelling shall be outside the camp." Leviticus 13:46.

People have been inspired by something they read in the Bible, leading to amazing discoveries. Take Matthew Maury (1806–1873), a naval officer, who noticed the expression "paths of the sea" in Psalm 8.

  "...You have put all things under his feet, ...the birds of the heavens, and the fish of the sea, whatever passes along the paths of the seas." Psalm 8:6-8.

Until the 1800s, people believed that the sea was just a vast mass of water; how could it have "paths"? Maury took God at His word and went looking for them. By plotting the sightings of whales and noting their harpoon scars, he confirmed he was seeing the same individuals in both the Atlantic and Pacific oceans. This, along with his research into the ocean currents and winds, led to the discovery of the most efficient routes for shipping. Two of his books, still in print today, are definitive volumes:

- Investigations Of The Winds And Currents Of The Sea.
- Sailing Directions.

For Christians, the primary purpose of the entire Bible is to reveal Christ. Therefore, it ultimately draws its authority from the fact that it truly speaks of God and his Son. This section does not suggest that proving these scientific facts proves the Bible is reliable. Instead, it is because God is the inspiration behind the Bible that he has and will continue to reveal facts behind his creation.

Internal consistency in the Bible

Despite many authors writing over centuries, the Bible has a remarkable consistency. The books interconnect and create a coherent narrative with a single message.

The fulfilment of prophecies also points to a case for the divine inspiration behind the Bible. By looking at the 300 or so prophecies relating to Christ, we can see that they have all been fulfilled. Sceptics suggest that this was all coincidental. The statistician, Charles Ryrie, calculated that for the same person to fulfil just eight of these prophecies is 1 in 10^{17}. This fraction is infinitesimally small. A layperson would declare the chance of eight prophecies being fulfilled by chance is virtually impossible. (See Prophecies about The Messiah in Appendix E for some examples.)

The transformative power of the Bible

We cannot overestimate the impact of the Bible on people and nations. Many individuals testify to the effect of the

Bible's teaching on their lives. Nations have used the teachings and moral principles within it to influence their country's values and laws.

The miracle of the Bible's continued circulation

The fact that the Bible is still available to us today is a miracle in itself. It has been the subject of multiple attempts to destroy it. Roman Emperors, who outlawed it, thought they had burnt all known copies. Each generation produces groups who ridicule the Bible and its followers, and some who would like to see it outlawed completely.

Its circulation is also a miracle. Although no single version makes it to the top of the best-seller list, people widely accept the Bible as the best-selling book each year. On September 21st, 1522, Martin Luther's German version became a bestseller when he sold it at the Leipzig Fair.

The Bible is still a significant book. Many people have risked and continue to risk their lives to distribute the Bible. Authorities executed some early translators and modern-day smugglers for daring to make the Bible accessible to everyone.

We can see that the evidence above shows that our current Bible is based on the original scripts. Archaeological and historical records can ratify much of its contents. Christian belief goes further than this. It says that the Bible is the inspired word of God. God prompted the authors to write their books, giving them special revelations to write down in their own way. Sometimes, the authors are at pains to point out that God was not just interested in the concept being documented, but he was instrumental in the words themselves, for example:

> "Moses came and told the people all the words of the Lord and all the rules. And all the people answered with one voice and said, "All the words that the Lord has spoken we will do." And Moses wrote down all the words of the Lord." Exodus 24:3-4.

> "In the beginning of the reign of Jehoiakim the son of Josiah, king of Judah, this word came from the Lord: "Thus says the Lord: Stand in the court of the Lord's house, and speak to all the cities of Judah that come to worship in the house of the Lord all the words that I command you to speak to them; do not hold back a word." Jeremiah 26:1-2.

Jesus himself believed the Old Testament, which he often called "The Law and the Prophets":

> Jesus said, "...See that you say nothing to anyone, but go, show yourself to the priest and offer for your cleansing what Moses commanded, for a proof to them." Mark 1:44.

> "He answered them, "And why do you break the commandment of God for the sake of your tradition?"" Matthew 15:3.

> "For truly, I say to you, until heaven and earth pass away, not an iota, not a dot, will pass from the Law until all is accomplished." Matthew 5:18.

John Wenham, a 20th-century Bible scholar, agrees:

> "To [Jesus], Moses, the prophets, David and the other Scripture-writers were truly inspired men with a message given by the Spirit of God." Christ and the Bible (1972)

Dealing with inconsistency

You may have heard of the doctrine of biblical inerrancy. It asserts that the Bible is entirely without error or fault in all its teachings. This is based on the belief that God inspired the Bible and is, therefore, completely trustworthy and authoritative. Many Christians adhere to this doctrine as a fundamental aspect of their faith. I would add here that this can only be applied to the original manuscripts. Once man is involved in the translation process, some errors will occur, though not deliberately. In essence, the Bible is the word of God and he is still using it to speak the truth to us today.

As Christians, there is no middle option. Either all of it is believable, or none of it is. We cannot pick and choose what to accept. How would we decide what to keep and what to throw away? It does not mean that we can easily understand the Bible. It can seem to contradict itself in places. In the fifth century, Augustine, a notable Christian, said,

> "I most firmly believe that the authors [of scripture] were completely free from error. And if in these writings I am perplexed by anything which appears to me opposed to truth, I do not hesitate to suppose that either the [manuscript] is faulty or the translator has not caught the meaning of what was said, or I myself have failed to understand it."

When dealing with inconsistencies, remember that context is key. When was it written? Who was it written to? What was happening at the time? Not forgetting that the Old Testament is history, poetry and prophecy, each type needing a different approach. A common adage is, "The plain things are the main things, and the main things are the plain things". The Bible repeats its important messages and themes many times without contradicting each other. That which is less important appears less often. Do not put great emphasis on that which the Bible does not dwell on either.

How the Bible is Translated

When you go shopping for a book, be it fiction or non-fiction, you expect to find one or two versions available, maybe the latest revision in hardback or paperback. If you were to line up all the editions of a particular Charles Dickens novel, they may differ in shape, size and cover, but their contents would be almost identical. You could have a copy dated 1900 and know that someone with a 2000 version would be reading the same words. You could have an in-depth discussion about what you have read without the distraction of differing words. That might not be true if both of you were reading French versions of the book translated by different people.

This is where the Bible differs from almost all other books. Not many people are fluent in Old Testament Hebrew or New Testament Greek. Most cannot read the Bible in the original language, hence the need for a translation.

The process of translating is not just translating the words. Language is more than words. Their order is essential in making sense of what is being conveyed. Behind the words are cultural values, assumptions, habits, idioms and traditions. These do not always translate well, and readers who come from different backgrounds can miss the subtle meanings. Even the earliest English translations can now seem out of date, and their language feels old-fashioned.

Language is more than a series of words.

Languages have their limitations. Things that are important in a culture have many words. Take the concept of snow to an Inuit. They have at least 50 words to describe all its nuances. English has one.

There's a similar relationship between Biblical Greek and English. The English word 'love' is used as the translation of four distinct Greek words. Each one describes a different depth of love and the relationship between the people expressing it. Then there's the English word 'knowledge' or 'to know'. The equivalent words in Greek describe the type of knowledge and how the 'knower' received that knowledge, for example, by learning or by inspiration.

At the opposite end of the scale, a language can have one word with many meanings. The next complete edition of the Oxford English Dictionary (set for a 2037 release) is expected to have at least 645 meanings for the word 'run'.

Lastly, words are time-critical. Today, if you say something is awful, you are being unkind. However, in the past, it was a term that people used to praise things. It meant that someone or something was "worthy of awe."

At each point where a word or phrase could mean different things or a slightly different nuance, the translator has to make an interpretive decision. There are plenty of resources to help with the alternative translations. We take a look at them in Other Resources in Appendix F.

Whilst a translation can be accurate, it can fail to convey the poetic nature of some of the text. Often, in the Old Testament, the poetry rhymes or has a format where each line begins with the following letter of the alphabet. This gets lost in translation. Using a commentary can help point out when this occurs.

Today, multiple translations exist because of the complexity of language and meeting the needs of the reader. In most of the versions, the translations have started with the original language sources and are not reworked from an existing translation. A Bible's preface will tell you the approach the translators took and the readership they are trying to reach. Translators walk a tightrope between accuracy, understandability and readability. This results in three types of translation: word-for-word, thought-for-thought and paraphrase.

A word-for-word translation aims to give an accurate picture of the original writing, its form, grammar, meaning and structure. Translators alter the wording only if it would affect the intended meaning. This "getting the words right" approach lets the reader figure out the meaning of some verses for themselves.

A thought-for-thought translation is trying to get a sense of what was originally written. It conveys the original meaning in a readable way. This method creates a more fluent version than word-for-word, though it can lose some nuances.

The final method is the paraphrase. There is less emphasis on the original language. It explains the point or the bigger picture using modern idioms. This obscures the original text, so this translation is not suitable for deep study or for establishing doctrine.

When comparing the two primary methods:
- Word-for-word highlights repeated words that are close to each other. It translates them the same even if the sentence seems stilted. Thought-for-thought will change the repeated words when it makes for better reading.
- The literal translation of phrases makes it easier to look for other verses having the exact same words. In thought-for-thought, these connections are less obvious,

requiring other resources to find them.

- Word-for-word lets us see the subtleties in the original version, whereas thought-for-thought can give us a better sense of the whole passage.

There is no one perfect translation.

What Bible Translations are Available?

Having established what goes into translating the Bible, let us look at the most familiar translations.

Word-for-word

New American Standard Bible (NASB)

This translation is recognised as the most literal translation. It focuses on the original words rather than the thoughts behind them. It pays close attention to reflecting the same verb tenses as the original but is often difficult to understand.

> "And do not be conformed to this world, but be transformed by the renewing of your mind, so that you may prove what the will of God is, that which is good and acceptable and perfect." Romans 12:2 (NASB)

English Standard Version (ESV)

This translation tends towards the literal end of the scale. It focuses on following the structure of the original language whilst keeping the idioms.

> "Do not be conformed to this world, but be transformed by the renewal of your mind, that by testing you may discern what is the will of God, what is good and acceptable and perfect." Romans 12:2 (ESV)

King James Version (KJV) and New King James Version (NKJV)

The KJV, published in 1611, focuses on formal language and literal concepts. It is written in old English, which can make it difficult to understand. More modern non-KJV translations use earlier manuscripts than the ones used by the KJV translators. This explains how the KJV often has more verses than a newer translation.

The NKJV is an updated version, published in 1982, that replaces some of the outdated words.

> "And be not conformed to this world: but be ye transformed by the renewing of your mind, that ye may prove what is that good, and acceptable, and perfect, will of God." Romans 12:2 (KJV)

Thought-for-thought

Christian Standard Bible (CSB)

A translation that strikes a balance between literal and readable. It focuses on clarity for today's reader. In doing so, it uses more notes than found in other thought-for-thought Bibles.

> "Do not be conformed to this age, but be transformed by the renewing of your mind, so that you may discern what is the good, pleasing, and perfect will of God." Romans 12:2 (CSB)

New International Version (NIV)

A popular translation that tries to balance accuracy with readability. It provides more interpretation for difficult-to-understand passages.

> "Do not conform to the pattern of this world, but be transformed by the renewing of your mind. Then you will be able to test and approve what God's will is—

his good, pleasing and perfect will." Romans 12:2 (NIV)

Paraphrase

New Living Translation (NLT)

A translation that is easy to read. The translators tried to translate as simply yet literally as possible, which means they clarified complex or unfamiliar metaphors and terms. It is ideal for devotional time rather than deep study.

> "Don't copy the behavior and customs of this world, but let God transform you into a new person by changing the way you think. Then you will learn to know God's will for you, which is good and pleasing and perfect." Romans 12:2 (NLT)

The Message (MSG)

This translation was meant for easy reading and understanding, not for study. It uses modern American terminology to explain much of the scripture, which a British reader can find difficult to understand. It is important that this is not the sole translation that you use.

> "Don't become so well-adjusted to your culture that you fit into it without even thinking. Instead, fix your attention on God. You'll be changed from the inside out. Readily recognize what he wants from you, and quickly respond to it. Unlike the culture around you, always dragging you down to its level of immaturity, God brings the best out of you, develops well-formed maturity in you." Romans 12:2 (MSG)

Along with these translations, many other versions are freely available via online apps or electronic downloads.

You may come across another translation, the New World Bible, produced by the Jehovah's Witnesses. They believe that Jesus was a created being, inferior to God and not the

Messiah. Although their translation uses the same sources as the Christian Bible, it has been translated with that viewpoint in mind. It is especially notable that the New World Bible removes all verses about the Trinity and alters some passages to fit its teachings.

Another version to avoid is the Reader's Digest Bible, which cuts out about 55% of the Old Testament and another 25% of the New Testament, including Revelation 22:19, which says,

> "If anyone takes away from the words of the book of this prophecy, God will take away his share in the tree of life and in the holy city, which are described in this book."

How to Choose a Bible for Yourself

When choosing your Bible, there is no right and wrong choice. If you want to hear the sense of a passage, choose a thought-for-thought version, but if you are going to study a passage, then choose a word-for-word version. Comparing versions broadens your view of a passage and can help you understand it better.

You can read most Bible versions online, often with the option of showing two or more translations side by side. To start studying, I would recommend buying one version to have in your hand and using the internet for other translations.

One last thing to consider before taking the step of actually buying a Bible is what format to buy.

As you would expect, all translations come in a range of styles and sizes. The Bible offers more options: what else do you want in your copy? Some choices available are:

Standard – This version contains the Bible text with nothing added.

Cross-referenced – This version has notes that indicate where a verse either references or is referenced by another Bible text.

Journalling – This version can have a wide margin or blank pages. This is good for writing notes and reflections, as well as journaling and decorating.

Interlinear - A Bible that simply presents the Hebrew or Greek text alongside its English language translation.

Parallel - Parallel Bibles feature two translations of the Bible, side by side.

Study – This is a much bigger version. Each page has a cross-reference as well as notes to unpack the text. There is often a concordance at the back, as well as helpful illustrations, maps and tables.

The following picture shows a section of a study Bible, identifying some of the above features.

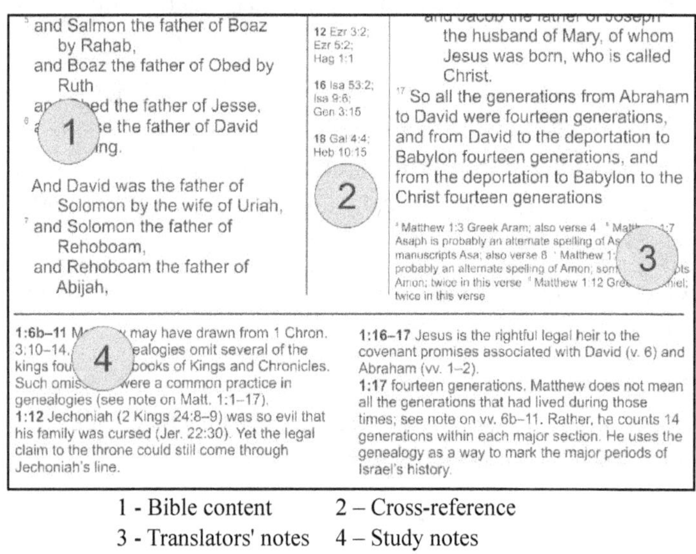

1 - Bible content   2 – Cross-reference
3 - Translators' notes   4 – Study notes

The most important point of having a Bible is to read it. Try not to get overwhelmed when making the choice. Speak to your friends and pastor for their recommendations. If you can afford it, buy a study Bible. Then, you can choose whether to read the study notes or just the text. Do not become over-reliant on the study notes, as you will gain more from doing your own research.

Reading and Studying the Bible

We have established that the Bible is the inspired Word of God and is good for encouraging Christians. It is a mixture of writings by numerous authors over many years. What is the best way to begin reading and studying it?

If you think back to studying a fiction book for an exam, the first instruction was to read it from beginning to end. This way, you will meet its characters, follow its plot, and gain insight into its themes. There was no point in dissecting the first chapter without knowing its place in the book.

The Bible is just the same, though many of us would baulk at the thought of reading it from cover to cover before diving in. This is achievable. It will take you about 75 hours to read it through. Alternatively, you could listen to someone reading it, much like a podcast - search 'audible Bible' on the internet. With a wide range of recordings available, you are likely to find a reader's voice that is easy to listen to.

Reading a simpler version can also give you a good grounding. Find yourself a copy of 'The Children's Bible in 365 Days' by Mary Batchelor (published by Lion). This is an easy way to grasp the key texts and meet the notable characters in the Bible. However, please don't take a year to read through it; a week or two should be plenty.

Once you have grasped an overview of the Bible, it is time to study it.

What is the purpose of studying the Bible?

If you have an interest in life - painting, gardening, history - you find yourself wanting to learn more about it. You will read books, watch programs and visit places. It is the same with the Bible. However, we are not just looking for more information about God and his plan for us; we want transformation. We have a desire to know and love God better. Through studying, we have the opportunity to learn more about God. As we apply his truth to our lives, it changes us and glorifies him.

The Bible tells us of his plan of redemption, his faithfulness to his people even when they're not faithful to him, and his constant love that tries to point us back to Himself. When we realise how much God loves us and how much he has done for us, especially in sending Jesus to become the ultimate sacrifice, we will want to worship him. He will become the focus of our lives. Transformation has no choice but to follow. We will love him with our hearts and minds. If we approach this the wrong way around – by trying to transform ourselves on our own - following God will become a burden, not a joy.

> The most important commandment is "'You shall love the Lord your God with all your heart and with all your soul and with all your mind and with all your strength.' The second is this, 'You shall love your neighbour as yourself.'" Mark 12:30-31.

Romans 12:1-2 adds to this when it says,

> "I appeal to you therefore, brothers, by the mercies of God, to present your bodies as a living sacrifice, holy and acceptable to God, which is your spiritual worship. Do not be conformed to this world but be transformed by the renewal of your mind, that by testing you may discern what is the will of God, what is good and acceptable and perfect."

Remember that the Bible is a living book. The God who inspired its writing is still inspiring us today as we read it and come to love its contents. Take time to listen to what he is saying to you as you read and study His Word.

Which Bible to use

As we saw earlier, there are plenty of versions to choose from. Pick a 'word-for-word' or 'thought-for-thought' translation. The former might be slightly harder to grasp, but being as accurate as possible, you won't miss anything. The latter gives you the overall gist of the passage. Try to use a "Study Version" of the Bible, which has annotations and helpful background information on each page.

A paraphrased version can be a way of seeing an alternative narrative for a passage, but it is not useful for studying.

Get ready to study

Preparing to study:

> Be purposeful: Set aside time to study. Fit it into your daily routine so that it becomes a natural thing to do. Studying and praying are as essential to us as eating. Many people schedule the time in their calendars. That way, it is more likely to get done. As you get into the habit, you will be encouraged to continue more often or for a more extended period of time.

Find a place:

> Have all your materials: Gather together your Bible plus a pen and paper. Some people also find highlighters useful for annotating their Bible and notes. Having a dictionary, concordance and Bible atlas would be helpful, although these can be online rather than physical copies. (See Other Resources in Appendix F)

Prepare your heart:

> Talk to God; tell him who he is to you and what he has done for you. Confess anything that needs confessing. Enter your study time peacefully so that there's nothing to block you from receiving revelation and inspiration.

How to approach a passage of scripture

Take the Bible seriously by being willing to spend time studying it.

Some passages are easy to understand, while others are complicated. Be honest with what you read. Be willing to listen to what it says rather than trying to make it mean what you want it to.

Do not 'cherry-pick' single verses to study. Always read passages in their context and with regard to their style (see Studying the Different Writing Styles on page 42). Scholars added the chapter/verse numbering and sub-headings to the original writing at a later date and are not seen as inspired. Indeed, they are often a distraction, especially when the thoughts of the author straddle a chapter break; for example, Paul's speech to the people in Jerusalem starts at Acts 21:37 and finishes at Acts 22:21.

How to study a passage

There are many documented ways to study the Bible, usually using acronyms to help you remember the steps. Here, we will use the simple steps of reading, observation, interpretation and application.

<u>Read</u> more than the passage you want to study so that you can see it in context. Read it more than once. I recommend reading it out loud. It can be strange at first, but the benefit of speaking every word slows you down and more than makes up for the initial embarrassment. Note if this passage

is part of a larger section. Did the author write about this topic across more than one chapter?

Now, look at what you <u>observe</u> in the passage.

Context is key. As a starting point, ask questions about the passage using who, what, when, where, how and why. For example:

- What happened before or after the passage?
- Where is it happening?
- Who is the author writing to?
- How do I handle the style in which it is written?

Note:

- Where the emphasis is.
- What is repeated?
- Words you don't understand.
- The order of ideas and thoughts.
- Look at the words in context; for example, is Jesus called Christ, Son of God, Redeemer? Think about why this is important.

Look at the relationship of ideas. Is there:

- A cause and effect, i.e. if this happens, then what are the consequences?

  "If any of you lacks wisdom, let him ask God, who gives generously to all without reproach, and it will be given him." James 1:5.

- A question that is asked and answered?

  "Good Teacher, what must I do to inherit eternal life? And Jesus said to him,...." Mark 10:17-18.

- A comparison, e.g.

  "The kingdom of heaven is like treasure hidden in a field." Matthew 13:44.

Is there anything you need help with? Now is the time to use the resources available. There are so many things that you could look up. To begin with, limit yourself to spending five or ten minutes. This will stop you from going down rabbit holes. Write down any questions you have for further research or to ask somebody in your church.

Moving on to <u>interpretation</u>. What does it mean? What does it tell me about God? What does it tell me about man?

The final task is <u>application</u>. What is my response? What do I need to ask God to help me with? Write down your thoughts, questions and revelations. What else do you want to follow up on?

What to study

The Bible is so big it can be difficult to know where to start. For a beginner, I suggest studying a gospel. Study the life and death of Christ in its original context. Use your resources to connect Christ to Old Testament prophecies.

Try the Gospel of Luke. Luke was a doctor and historian who wrote about Christ's life for his friend Theophilus. Theophilus knew little about Christ, so this gospel is a straightforward biography rather than having an underlying agenda, such as Matthew's need to prove to the Jews that Jesus was the Christ.

You could follow this up by studying Luke's Acts of the Apostles, a history of the early church. Luke had personal experience of travelling through Asia Minor with the first disciples.

Other options

As you get more comfortable studying the Bible, many options open up to you. You could study a person, a topic or a word. There are plenty of guided studies in book form or online. Ask around to see what other people have found useful. You will want to use something that encourages you to study the Bible for yourself rather than one that gives you all its answers.

Studying with other people is also beneficial. It allows you to ask your questions and learn from others. Group study adds another dimension but is not a substitute for your personal time with God.

Studying the
Different Writing Styles

The Bible contains many styles of writing. Understanding each one will help you to study a particular passage.

Old Testament Narrative

Genesis, Exodus, Numbers, Joshua, Judges, Ruth, 1 & 2 Samuel, 1 & 2 Kings, 1 & 2 Chronicles, Ezra, Nehemiah, Esther

A narrative tells an account of what happened. Nearly half of the Old Testament is considered narrative, covering the lives of God's people before Jesus' time. We read of what happened to them, from creation through the reigns of the judges and kings, their exile in Babylon before their return to Jerusalem.

You will gain much from reading these accounts. The authors tell of the ups and downs of life and how ordinary people are prone to walk away from God. All the smaller events link together to create a complete account of creation, the Fall, redemption and restoration.

These writings help us relate to a faithful God, who has a never-ending love for his people, carrying out His plan of redemption throughout history.

When studying the stories, you could consider:
- What is the essence of this account?
- What did the people do? How did God respond? What was his purpose?
- What does this tell us about the character of God?
- Where does this fit into the bigger picture?

- Does it point to Jesus? If so, how?
- What can I learn from the mistakes and progress of the Biblical characters?
- What would the original audience have understood that I miss because of cultural differences?

Law

Genesis, Exodus, Leviticus, Numbers and Deuteronomy

Although these first five books contain narrative sections, they are known as "The Law". God gave the rules, statutes and instructions to the Israelites through Moses. These laid out the way people were to live and to treat their neighbours. They also laid out the conditions of God's covenant with the nation of Israel.

God's concern was to create a healthy, functioning community. This included the upholding of justice, the treatment of the poor and outsiders, and the way in which the people remained healthy. Above all, God wanted these same things for his relationship with his people, providing a way for people to live in harmony with him as well. Jesus came to fulfil the Law and introduce a new way of approaching God through grace and forgiveness. Understanding the Law helps us see our need for Jesus and the transformative power of the New Covenant.

When studying the Law, you could consider:
- What is the purpose of the particular law?
- What does this law show us about God's character and his desire for His people?
- What happened when the Israelites failed to obey this law?
- Do we see Jesus upholding, expanding or fulfilling this law in the New Testament? If so, how?

Poetry

Psalms, Song of Solomon, Book of Lamentations

These are the prayers and songs sung to God.

The Psalms had a rhythm and structure that helped people remember God's Word when oral history was the primary way of handing down stories and memories. They were usually written from the heart rather than from a factual viewpoint. Their content is unusual in that they are speaking to or about God, without God replying.

There are Psalms for different occasions, including praise, thanksgiving, lament and wisdom. We find that we can relate to their experiences and emotions. We rejoice with them in their rejoicing or take comfort from them when we are having a tough time.

The Book of Lamentations is a series of poetic laments. They express deep sorrow, grief, and remorse over the events that led to the destruction of Jerusalem and the exile of its people. It is a poignant reflection on the consequences of sin and the enduring faithfulness of God in times of hardship.

The Song of Solomon celebrates the beauty of love and desire between a bride and groom. The relationship between the bride and groom is often interpreted as an allegory of God's love for his people.

Today, these writings help us relate to God in a real and authentic way. They can be the starting point for our worship and prayers.

When studying the books of poetry, you could consider:
- What were the circumstances that provoked its writing? A cross-reference or study guide will point you to the relevant narrative passage.
- What type of poetry is it, e.g. praise, lament, and how

was it used at the time?
- What picture does it paint?
- How does it speak to us today?
- How can we use it in our quiet time with God?

Wisdom

Job, Proverbs, Ecclesiastes

These books are collections of writings designed to shape the moral and ethical lives of the reader. They offer God's perspective on the practical aspects of daily living.

Job's laments look at what he thought and believed in the light of his unexpected circumstances.

Proverbs contains short sayings and deals with generalisations.

Ecclesiastes explores the search for meaning and the way to respond to it.

Books in this literary style help direct our hearts and actions in everything we encounter in our lives and, most importantly, teach us how to have awe and reverence for God.

When studying the wisdom books, you could consider:
- How is this message providing guidance? How does it debate the meaning or purpose of life?
- What did I learn that I can apply to my life today?

Old Testament Prophecy

Isaiah, Jeremiah, Ezekiel, Daniel, Hosea, Joel, Amos, Obadiah, Jonah, Micah, Nahum, Habakkuk, Zephaniah, Haggai, Zechariah, Malachi

The prophecy books tell of God's attempts to bring the Israelites back into the right relationship with him. He spoke to many prophets throughout the Israelites' history, sixteen of whom have books named after them.

Much of the content is harsh, but it is easy to see that God is upholding his side of the Covenant contract with his people, even though they don't seem to care that they have broken their side. We see a God who loves his people and wants to draw them back to himself, much like he is doing with us today.

God also used prophets to foretell specific future events that would come to pass, which included God's rescue plan that would save the world. We can see the fulfilment of many of the prophecies in the Old and New Testaments.

When studying the prophecy books, you could consider:
- How would the original audience have read and understood this prophecy?
- How is the prophecy encouraging or disciplining the reader?
- What do I learn about God and what He wants from me?
- How is Jesus revealed in this prophecy?

Gospels

Matthew, Mark, Luke, John

These books are narratives. Unlike the Old Testament narratives, where Moses documented the oral histories passed down through the generations, the New Testament authors are believers who write down first-hand accounts.

They write about Christ's life, death and resurrection, as well as his teachings and miracles. Each writer had their own reasons for writing, but when read together, their accounts collectively testify to the same figure of Jesus.

- Mark and Luke assume the reader knows little about Christ.
- Matthew writes to the Jews to persuade them to see Christ as the Messiah.

- John writes to the Greeks to appeal to their logical and rational thinking.

When studying the gospels, you could consider:
- Who was the author writing to? What should I know about their culture?
- What do I learn about the way Jesus relates to people?
- Which Old Testament prophecies are being fulfilled in this passage?

Parables

Jesus used 40 parables in the Bible as stories and illustrations to communicate a message. They are often about the nature of the kingdom of God, how to respond to Jesus' ministry and how to live a loving life.

The parables encourage people to think and ask questions. We can do the same today and ask God to give us a fresh perspective on what he is doing.

When studying the parables, you could consider:
- How would the original audience have heard this parable?
- What cultural points of the time are referenced?
- What is the point Jesus is trying to make?
- Try retelling the parable for today's reader.

New Testament Narrative

Acts of the Apostles

This narrative follows the early growth of the Christian church after the death and resurrection of Jesus Christ. It documents the coming of the Holy Spirit at Pentecost, who empowered the apostles to spread the message of Jesus to various regions. It follows the journeys of Peter, Paul, and Barnabas, who faced persecution and opposition as they preached the gospel and established new Christian communities. Overall, the book emphasises the power of the Holy Spirit, the importance of faith in Jesus Christ, and the unity of believers in the early Christian church.

When studying the Acts of the Apostles, you could consider:
- How did the apostles face their challenges?
- What role did the Holy Spirit play in the lives of the apostles?
- How did the apostles handle persecution and opposition while spreading the message of Christ?
- How did the apostles' experiences influence the early development of the Christian church?
- What can the apostles teach me about leadership and unity among Christians?
- How did the apostles navigate cultural and religious differences when spreading the Gospel?

Letters

Romans, 1 & 2 Corinthians, Galatians, Ephesians, Philippians, Colossians, 1 & 2 Thessalonians, 1 & 2 Timothy, Titus, Philemon, Hebrews, James, 1 & 2 Peter, 1, 2 & 3 John, Jude

In the first century AD, the twenty-one letters (also called epistles) were written by the apostles to the early Christians and churches. They explained Jesus' new covenant and corrected misunderstandings.

In the letters, there is often only one side of the conversation. When the letters address particular issues or points of doctrine in the early church, it is possible to think that one letter contradicts another. But looking at the different contexts, everything becomes clear.

Although each letter acknowledges one recipient, a church or a person, it would have been passed to the neighbouring churches.

When studying the letters, you could consider:
- Reading the entire letter to get the gist of the arguments.
- What instruction was given, and why was it needed?
- What cultural truths belong to the first century? Which truths are still relevant today? Try to explore this objectively. There will often be truths that you would rather were not relevant today.

New Testament Prophecy

Revelation

This is the last book in the New Testament and the Bible. It is prophetic in nature. Unlike most Old Testament prophecies, it is waiting to be fulfilled. In very symbolic language, it tells of the triumph of good over evil and provides hope and victory to those of us who are in Christ.

When studying this prophecy, you could consider:
- What conflict do you notice between good and evil?
- How does God triumph over evil and Satan?
- How is God's sovereignty revealed?

An Example of a Bible Study

Let us take a look at the Gospel of Luke, chapter 1.

As we are at the beginning of a book, we will start by researching the context. Use your study Bible or commentary to read about Luke and his Gospel.

<u>Author</u> – Historians believe that Luke wrote this book and the Acts of the Apostles. They think he was gentile by birth, well-educated in Greek culture and a physician. He accompanied Paul on some of his travels. 2 Timothy 4: 9-11 shows him to be a loyal friend.

> "Do your best to come to me soon. For Demas, in love with this present world, has deserted me and gone to Thessalonica. Crescens has gone to Galatia, Titus to Dalmatia. Luke alone is with me."

<u>Recipients</u> - Theophilus (his name means one who loves God) was the intended recipient. The reference to him as "most excellent" would lead one to conclude that he was real. There is speculation that he was Luke's patron and provided funds for the copying and distribution of the gospel.

<u>Purpose</u> - Luke wanted to document what he knew about Jesus based on his travels with the first disciples and Paul. Luke emphasises that Jesus' message was for the gentiles as well as the Jews. Expect to find facts with little background.

<u>Content</u> - the book starts from Jesus' birth and finishes at his resurrection. Luke wants the reader to understand the way to salvation. He includes many of the incidents seen in the other

Gospels. Luke emphasises the way Jesus lived his life, writing about his many prayers, miracles and parables. Luke devotes three chapters to describing Jesus' birth, fifteen chapters to recounting his ministry and the final six chapters to documenting his death and resurrection.

The first chapter of Luke is long. We will confine ourselves to studying the introduction in verses 1 to 4 and the foretelling of John the Baptist's birth in verses 5 to 25.

Luke 1: 1 - 4

<u>Observation</u> - This formal introduction shows how Luke recorded and wrote the gospel. He has checked his sources. He wants the reader to have a firm foundation for what he believes.

- Who was Theophilus? (commentary or Bible dictionary)
- Who else was called 'most excellent'? (concordance)

<u>Interpretation</u> - The reader can be sure that Luke is a trustworthy author. If his writings had been false, the objectors of the time would have raised their voices in protest. They would have stopped the distribution of this gospel.

Think about the oral traditions passed down through your family. I expect members correct one another's recounted stories if they think they are inaccurate.

<u>Application</u> - Thank God for Luke's gospel. Thank him for what you will learn about God from reading and studying it.

Luke 1: 5- 25

<u>Observation</u> - Zechariah and Elizabeth were from Aaron's line. They walked in God's ways, not sinless but following God's ordinances. Zechariah was chosen by lot to replenish the incense in the temple.

The angel's message to Zechariah was specific, revealing John's name, character, and purpose. Zechariah's unbelief led to him becoming dumb. The crowds saw a different Zechariah when he came out of the temple and knew he had seen God.

Elizabeth fell pregnant and stayed hidden for five months. She praised God because he had shown her his favour and taken away her disgrace.

Questions you could answer to help your study:

- What is the line of Aaron? (commentary or concordance)
- What does it mean to be chosen by lot? (dictionary)
- What was Zechariah doing in the temple? What is the significance of the incense? (commentary)
- How are Zechariah and Elizabeth's responses different?
- What was the Old Testament prophecy about Elijah coming back? Read Malachi 4:5-6.
- Who else was barren before giving birth? How did this help Elizabeth believe? Read Genesis 11:30, Genesis 25:21, Genesis 29:31, 1 Samuel 1&2, Judges 13.
- Why might Luke have included this narrative before the foretelling of Jesus' birth?

<u>Interpretation</u> - What does it tell us about God?

- People can come into his presence.
- He can orchestrate what he wants to. Zachariah was chosen by lot at the appointed time. There was no guarantee that he might ever have been selected.
- God has a plan and purpose for everyone (see the angel's description of John). Read Psalm 139.
- God is the God of miracles.

What does this passage tell us about man?

- Man can follow all God's rules and still not trust him in

everything.

- God can use ordinary people for his purposes.
- We can be hampered for a while if we choose to disbelieve what God has said.

<u>Application -</u> What is God trying to get your attention for?

Thank God for sending John to point the way to Christ. Thank him for being in control of everything, including your life. Ask him where you need to trust him. Ask him to help you come to enter his presence. You do not need to wait for your chance.

Going Forward

Now, it is time to practice what you have learnt in these chapters.

May you be blessed by studying the Bible. Ask God what he has for you to learn and appropriate for yourself.

If you would like to download some bible study templates based on the method in this book, go to karenrizzi.co.uk/resources

Every blessing

Karen

Appendix A
Book Name Abbreviations

Below, the books of the Bible are presented in alphabetical order, along with their usual abbreviated names. The OT/NT column shows which Testament the book is found in, alongside its position. The final column shows the book's style.

Abbreviation	Book Title	OT/NT	Style
1 Ch. or 1 Chr.	1 Chronicles	OT 13	Narrative
1 Cor.	1 Corinthians	NT 7	Letter
1 Jn	1 John	NT 23	Letter
1 Kings	1 Kings	OT 11	Narrative
1 Pet.	1 Peter	NT 21	Letter
1 Sam.	1 Samuel	OT 9	Narrative
1 Thess.	1 Thessalonians	NT 13	Letter
1 Tim.	1 Timothy	NT 15	Letter
2 Ch. or 2 Chr.	2 Chronicles	OT 14	Narrative
2 Cor.	2 Corinthians	NT 8	Letter
2 Jn.	2 John	NT 24	Letter
2 Kings	2 Kings	OT 12	Narrative
2 Pet.	2 Peter	NT 22	Letter
2 Sam.	2 Samuel	OT 10	Narrative

2 Thess.	2 Thessalonians	NT 14	Letter
2 Tim.	2 Timothy	NT 16	Letter
3 Jn.	3 John	NT 25	Letter
Acts	Acts	NT 5	Narrative
Amos	Amos	OT 30	Prophecy
Col.	Colossians	NT 12	Letter
Dan.	Daniel	OT 27	Prophecy
Deut.	Deuteronomy	OT 5	Law
Eccles.	Ecclesiastes	OT 21	Wisdom
Eph.	Ephesians	NT 10	Letter
Est.	Esther	OT 17	Narrative
Ex.	Exodus	OT 2	Law
Ezek.	Ezekiel	OT 26	Prophecy
Ezra	Ezra	OT 15	Prophecy
Gal.	Galatians	NT 9	Letter
Gen.	Genesis	OT 1	Law
Hab.	Habakkuk	OT 35	Prophecy
Hag.	Haggai	OT 37	Prophecy
Heb.	Hebrews	NT 19	Letter
Hos.	Hosea	OT 28	Prophecy
Isa.	Isaiah	OT 23	Prophecy
James	James	NT 20	Letter
Jer.	Jeremiah	OT 24	Prophecy
Jn.	John	NT 4	Gospel
Job	Job	OT 18	Narrative
Joel	Joel	OT 29	Prophecy
Jonah	Jonah	OT 32	Prophecy

Appendix A: Book Name Abbreviations

Josh.	Joshua	OT 6	Narrative
Jude	Jude	NT 26	Letter
Judg.	Judges	OT 7	Narrative
Lam.	Lamentations	OT 25	Wisdom
Lev.	Leviticus	OT 3	Law
Lk.	Luke	NT 3	Gospel
Mal.	Malachi	OT 39	Prophecy
Matt.	Matthew	NT 1	Gospel
Mic.	Micah	OT 33	Prophecy
Mk.	Mark	NT 2	Gospel
Nah.	Nahum	OT 34	Prophecy
Neh.	Nehemiah	OT 16	Narrative
Num.	Numbers	OT 4	Law
Obad.	Obadiah	OT 31	Prophecy
Phil.	Philippians	NT 11	Letter
Philem.	Philemon	NT 18	Letter
Prov.	Proverbs	OT 20	Wisdom
Ps.	Psalms	OT 19	Poetry
Rev.	Revelation	NT 27	Prophecy
Rom.	Romans	NT 6	Letter
Ruth	Ruth	OT 8	Narrative
Song	Song of Solomon	OT 22	Poetry
Titus	Titus	NT 17	Letter
Zech.	Zechariah	OT 38	Prophecy
Zeph.	Zephaniah	OT 36	Prophecy

Appendix B
Old Testament Timeline

Below, the books of the Old Testament are presented in their Biblical order, along with the dates when the events they refer to happened. The final column shows when the book was written.

All dates are based on the latest findings.

Book	Summary	Events occurred	Book Written
Genesis	The story of the world's creation and the Israelite people's beginnings.	4000-1800 BC	1450-1410 BC
Exodus	The Israelites' escape from slavery in Egypt and the receiving of the Ten Commandments.	1800-1445 BC	1450-1410 BC
Leviticus	A book of laws and regulations for the Israelites to follow in their worship and daily lives.	1445 BC	1445-1405 BC
Numbers	The Israelites' journey through the wilderness and the organisation of their community.	1445-1407 BC	1445-1405 BC
Deuteronomy	A recap of the earlier laws and more instructions for the Israelites before entering the Promised Land.	1407-1406 BC	1445-1405 BC
Joshua	The conquest of Canaan and the division of the land among the twelve tribes of Israel.	1406-1375 BC	1350-1200 BC
Judges	Stories of the Israelite judges who led the people during times of crisis.	1375-1075 BC	1050-1000 BC

APPENDIX B: OLD TESTAMENT TIMELINE

Ruth	A story of loyalty and faithfulness during a time of tragedy.	1140 BC	1000-950 BC
1 Samuel	The rise of King Saul and his eventual fall from grace.	1100-1010 BC	930-540 BC
2 Samuel	The reign of King David and the establishment of the kingdom of Israel.	1010-970 BC	930-540 BC
1 Kings	The reigns of King Solomon and subsequent kings of Israel and Judah.	970-853 BC	930-540 BC
2 Kings	The decline and fall of the kingdoms of Israel and Judah.	852-742 BC	930-540 BC
1 Chronicles	A genealogical record of the descendants of Israel's tribes and the reign of King David.	1003-970 BC	450-430 BC
2 Chronicles	A detailed account of the reign of King Solomon and the subsequent kings of Judah.	967-742 BC	450-430 BC
Ezra	The return of the exiled Israelites to their homeland and the rebuilding of the temple in Jerusalem.	537-456 BC	450-400 BC
Nehemiah	The rebuilding of the walls of Jerusalem and the restoration of the city.	445-432 BC	450-400 BC
Esther	The story of Queen Esther and her brave actions to save her people from destruction.	483-472 BC	450-350 BC
Job	A poetic exploration of suffering, faith, and the mystery of God's ways.	Before 2100 BC	600-400 BC
Psalms	A collection of songs and prayers expressing a range of emotions and experiences.	1407-580 BC	1000–500 BC

Proverbs	Wise sayings and advice for living a good and righteous life.	950 BC	950-700 BC
Ecclesiastes	Reflections on the meaninglessness of life and the importance of fearing God.	937 BC	450-200 BC
Song of Solomon	A love poem celebrating the beauty and intensity of human love.	950 BC	950-350 BC
Isaiah	Prophecies about the coming Messiah and messages of hope and restoration for Israel.	739-680 BC	740-680 BC
Jeremiah	Warnings of judgment and calls for repentance to the people of Judah.	627-586 BC	626-586 BC
Lamentations	Poems of sorrow and mourning over the destruction of Jerusalem.	586 BC	586 BC
Ezekiel	Visionary prophecies and messages of hope for the exiled Israelites.	593-586 BC	593-573 BC
Daniel	Stories of Daniel and his friends in exile, along with prophecies of future events.	605-539 BC	605-530 BC
Hosea	A metaphorical depiction of God's relationship with Israel as that of a faithful husband and unfaithful wife.	753 BC	750-715 BC
Joel	A call to repentance and a promise of restoration for Israel.	835 BC	830-800 BC
Amos	Warnings of judgment on Israel for their societal injustices and oppressions.	766 BC	760-750 BC
Obadiah	Prophecies of judgment against the neighbouring nations of Israel.	853 BC	586-520 BC

Jonah	The story of Jonah's reluctant mission to the city of Nineveh and God's mercy on the repentant people.	760 BC	780-760 BC
Micah	Messages of judgment against Israel for their sins and injustices, along with promises of restoration.	735 BC	735-700 BC
Nahum	Prophecies of judgment against the city of Nineveh.	697 BC	663-612 BC
Habakkuk	A dialogue between the prophet and God about the problem of evil and God's sovereignty.	625 BC	610-605 BC
Zephaniah	Warnings of judgment on Judah and promises of restoration for the remnant.	638 BC	630-620 BC
Haggai	Prophecies urging the people to rebuild the temple and return to faithful worship.	520 BC	520-510 BC
Zechariah	Visions of restoration and renewal for Jerusalem and the people of Israel.	520 BC	520-480 BC
Malachi	Messages of rebuke and encouragement to the people of Israel to remain faithful to God.	430 BC	450-400 BC

Appendix C
New Testament Timeline

Below is a timeline of the New Testament giving a date when the events happened and in which book you will find the narrative.

1 BC	Birth of John the Baptist	Luke 1
AD 1	Birth of Jesus	Matthew 1-2 Luke 2
AD 30 – 33	Jesus teaches and travels around Judea and Galilee	Matthew 3 – 18 Mark 1 – 10 Luke 3 – 17 John 1-11
AD 33	Jesus enters Jerusalem	Matthew 19 – 26 Mark 11 – 13 Luke 18 – 22 John 12-18
AD 33	The betrayal, crucifixion and resurrection of Jesus	Matthew 27 – 28 Mark 14-16 Luke 23-24 John 19-21
AD 33	The Ascension	Acts 1
	The Holy Spirit comes at Pentecost	Acts 2 – 12
AD 45	James writes his letter	James
AD 48	Paul's first missionary journey	Acts 13 – 18
AD 51	Paul writes to the Thessalonians	1 Thessalonians
AD 51	Paul writes to the Galatians	Galatians
AD 52	Paul writes to the Thessalonians again	2 Thessalonians
AD 54	Paul goes to Ephesus	Acts 19

	Paul writes to the Corinthians	1 Corinthians
AD 57	Paul visits Macedonia and Greece	Acts 20
	Paul writes to the Romans	Romans
	Paul writes to the Corinthians again	2 Corinthians
	Paul returns to Jerusalem	Acts 21 – 28
AD 60	Paul writes to the Ephesians	Ephesians
	Paul writes to the Colossians	Colossians
	Paul writes to Philemon	Philemon
AD 61	Paul writes to the Philippians	Philippians
AD 63	Paul writes to Timothy	1 Timothy
AD 64	Peter writes his first letter	1 Peter
AD 66	Paul writes to Titus	Titus
AD 67	Paul writes to Timothy again	2 Timothy
	Peter writes his second letter	2 Peter
AD 68	Letter to the Hebrews is written	Hebrews
	Jude writes his letter	Jude
AD 85 - 95	John writes his first letter	1 John
	John writes his second letter	2 John
	John writes his third letter	3 John
AD 90 - 95	John's Revelation on Patmos	Revelation

The Gospels and the Acts of the Apostles are challenging to date with precision. The table below shows the earliest and latest dates put forward by scholars.

However, many suggest the latest date of writing is 70 AD. This coincides with the fall of the temple in Jerusalem. Matthew's Gospel, in chapter 24, predicts this will happen.

None of the Gospels refer to the temple's destruction as having occurred.

	Earliest Date	Latest Date
Matthew	AD 50	AD 70
Mark	AD 55	AD 69
Luke	AD 60	AD 80
John	AD 50	AD 85
Acts of the Apostles	AD 63	AD 70

Appendix D
Comparison of the Gospels

This chart shows what each Gospel covers and where to find similar accounts in the other Gospels.

		Matt	Mark	Luke	John
1 BC	Birth of John the Baptist			Ch 1	
	Birth of Jesus	Ch 1		Ch 2	
AD 1	Visit of the Magi	Ch 2			
	Early life of Jesus				Ch 1
AD 30	John the Baptist prepares the way	Ch 3	Ch 1	Ch 3	
	Temptations of Jesus	Ch 4		Ch 4	
	Jesus calls the 12 disciples			Ch 5	
	Wedding at Cana				Ch 2
	Jesus and Nicodemus				Ch 3
	Jesus and the woman at the well				Ch 4
	Sermon on the Mount	Ch 5–7			
AD 31	Jesus ministers in Galilee	Ch 8	Ch 2		
	Jesus heals at the Pool of Bethesda				Ch 5
	Jesus heals on the Sabbath	Ch 12	Ch 3	Ch 6	
	Jesus answers John's disciples	Ch 11		Ch 7	

	Jesus tells many parables	Ch 13	Ch 4	Ch 8	
	Jesus heals a demoniac		Ch 5		
	Jesus heals a paralytic	Ch 9			
AD 32	Jesus sends out the 12 Disciples	Ch 10			
	Death of John the Baptist	Ch 14	Ch 6		
	Jesus feeds the 5,000			Ch 9	Ch 6
	Jesus teaches about clean and unclean items	Ch 15	Ch 7		
	Peter's confession of Christ	Ch 16	Ch 8		
	The Transfiguration	Ch 17	Ch 9		
	Jesus teaches on the greatest and least in the kingdom	Ch 18			
	Jesus teaches at the Feast of Tabernacles				Ch 7 – 10
AD 33	Jesus tells more parables			Ch 12 – 17	
	Jesus raises Lazarus				Ch 11
	Jesus' final journey to Jerusalem	Ch 19 – 20	Ch 10	Ch 18	
	Jesus' triumphal entry into Jerusalem	Ch 21	Ch 11	Ch 19	Ch 12 – 13
	Closing Ministry in Jerusalem	Ch 22 – 25	Ch 12 – 13	Ch 20 – 21	
	Jesus comforts his disciples				Ch 14 – 17
	Jesus' Last Supper, betrayal, trial and crucifixion	Ch 26-27	Ch 14 – 15	Ch 22 – 23	Ch 18 – 19
	Jesus' resurrection	Ch 28	Ch 16	Ch 24	Ch 20 – 21

Appendix E
Prophecies about The Messiah

Prophecy about Jesus	Where the prophecy is found	Where the prophecy is fulfilled
Born of a virgin	Isaiah 7:14	Matthew 1:23
Descendant of Abraham	Genesis 12:3	Matthew 1:1
From the tribe of Judah	Genesis 49:10	Luke 3:33
Born in Bethlehem	Micah 5:2	Matthew 2:1
Offered gifts as a child	Isaiah 60:6	Matthew 2:11
Called out of Egypt	Hosea 11:1	Matthew 2:15
Anointed with the Spirit of God	Isaiah 61:1	Matthew 3:16-17
Great preacher	Isaiah 61:1-2	Luke 4:17-21
Healed the sick	Isaiah 35:5-6	Matthew 11:4-6
Cast out demons	Isaiah 42:7	Matthew 12:22-24
Spoke in parables	Psalm 78:2	Matthew 13:34-35
Rejected by his own people	Isaiah 53:3	John 1:11
Rode into Jerusalem on a donkey	Zechariah 9:9	Matthew 21:5
Cleansed the temple	Malachi 3:1	Matthew 21:12-13
Betrayed by a friend	Psalm 41:9	Matthew 26:14-16

Betrayed by a close companion	Psalm 55:12-14	Matthew 26:47-50
Sold for 30 pieces of silver	Zechariah 11:12	Matthew 26:15
30 pieces of silver thrown in the temple	Zechariah 11:13	Matthew 27:5
Accused by false witnesses	Psalm 35:11	Matthew 26:59-61
Silent before his accusers	Isaiah 53:7	Matthew 27:12-14
Struck on the cheek	Micah 5:1	Matthew 27:30
Spit upon and mocked	Isaiah 50:6	Matthew 26:67
Lots cast for his clothing	Psalm 22:18	John 19:23-24
Crucified with criminals	Isaiah 53:12	Matthew 27:38
Pierced in his hands and feet	Psalm 22:16	John 20:25-27
Mocked and scorned	Psalm 22:7-8	Matthew 27:39-44
Wounded and bruised for our sins	Isaiah 53:5	John 19:1
Given gall and vinegar	Psalm 69:21	Matthew 27:34
Given vinegar to drink	Psalm 69:21	Matthew 27:34
None of his bones were broken	Psalm 34:20	John 19:33-36
Buried in a rich man's tomb	Isaiah 53:9	Matthew 27:57-60
Raised from the dead	Psalm 16:10	Matthew 28:5-7
Ascended to heaven	Psalm 68:18	Acts 1:9
Seated at the right hand of God	Psalm 110:1	Hebrews 10:12
Coming again in glory	Zechariah 14:4	Matthew 24:30
Interceding for his people	Isaiah 53:12	Romans 8:34
Offered as a sacrifice for sin	Isaiah 53:5	1 Peter 2:24
Justified many through his righteousness	Isaiah 53:11	Romans 5:18-19

Appendix F
Other Resources

Using extra resources can deepen your understanding of the Bible and aid in personal reflection and spiritual growth.

These resources are available in print or online. A Study Bible includes much of this material as part of its features.

A Biblical dictionary

A Biblical dictionary is a reference book that offers detailed explanations and definitions of words, terms, people, places, and concepts found in the Bible. These dictionaries often provide historical background, cultural context, and theological insights to help readers interpret and apply the teachings of the Bible. It can be a valuable tool for better understanding the text.

FIG, FIG TREE The fig tree is a significant fruit-bearing tree in the Holy Land. In the Bible, it is mentioned that Adam and Eve used its leaves to make clothing (Gen 3:7). Jesus once cursed a fig tree for not bearing fruit (Mark 11:13-14, 20-21). Visit the Plants section for more information.

FIGUREHEAD The emblem on the front of a ship known as a figurehead is mentioned in Acts 28:11 in various translations (NIV, NRSV, NASB). In this reference, the figure is depicted as the Twin Brothers Castor and Pollux, who are the sons of Zeus and Leda and associated with the constellation Gemini. Observing this constellation was seen as a positive

A Commentary

MATTHEW 20:1-34

Summary: The apostles have the authority to judge Israel. Those who give up material possessions will receive blessings many times over and eternal life. Despite the promises of abundant rewards, it is emphasized that attitudes are important, and those who seem to be first may end up last, while the last may end up first.

Matthew 20:1-16 - The Parable of the Labourers, emphasizes Jesus' lessons on genuine Christian service and wealth. In this parable, Christ is depicted as the householder and the Master of the vineyard, symbolizing the field of labor in service to the world.

In the morning, the first labourers were hired at dawn and offered a denarius, equivalent to a day's wage. The individuals idling in the marketplace were not being lazy; they were actively seeking employment. The householder then selected some workers from this group.

New workers were hired at 9 a.m., noon, 3

A Biblical commentary providing insights, explanations, historical context, and theological reflections on the passages of the Bible. They can help you understand the meaning of the text, its cultural background, and its relevance to contemporary life. There are many types of biblical commentary, including academic, devotional, historical, and theological perspectives.

A Concordance

WEAK

Judg	16:7	I shall become w
Ps	72:13	He has pity on the w
Ezek	34:4	strengthened the w
Mt	26:41	flesh is w.
Acts	20:35	we must support the w.
Rom	14:1	w in faith,
1 Cor	1:27	God chose what is w
2 Cor	2:10	whenever I am w,
Gal	4:9	turn back again to the w,
1 Thess	5:14	help the w.
Heb	7:18	because it was w.

WEALTH

Deut	8:17	have gotten me this w.
2 Chr	1:11	w. honour,
Ps	49:6	trust in their w.
Prov	13:7	yet have great w,
Eccl	5:10	nor the lover of w,
Song	8:7	all the w of his house.
Mt	13:22	lure of w.
Lk	16:11	dishonest w,
Rev	5:12	receive power and w.

WEEP (ING)

A concordance is a tool that helps you locate specific Bible words or phrases. For each word, it provides a list of verses where you will find the word in the Bible. Concordances can help you study specific themes, topics, or words and better understand their usage and context.

Appendix G
This is Salvation

Salvation is the freedom from the punishment for our sins (wrong-doings) and the promise of Eternal Life.

God wants a relationship with us. Because of our sin, we cannot enter his presence. We are not perfect. We can act out of wrong motives and do not always love our neighbour. This behaviour is not acceptable to God. Although he is loving, he is also just and righteous. We fall short of his standards.

In the Old Testament, God set up a system of animal sacrifices as a substitution for sin. By performing the sacrifice, a person became 'sinless' until they committed the next sin. People often forgot to perform the sacrifices and went their own way. God was forever calling them back to himself, only for them to fall away again.

God, in his love and great mercy towards us, sent Jesus to Earth as the promised Messiah or Saviour. He taught about God and his Kingdom. The leaders persecuted him and sentenced him to die on the cross. In his dying, he took all our sins with him and became our ultimate sacrifice. Three days after his death, he came back to life (the Resurrection), living on earth until he ascended to heaven to be seated with the Father.

If we agree that we cannot enter God's presence because of our sins and accept his sacrifice on our behalf, we are made right with God. We have an eternal relationship with him. We do not need any other sacrifices. God gives his Holy Spirit to dwell within us, helping us understand the Bible and live according to His principles and promises.

It is often said that Jesus would have died for me if I were the only one alive. The other side of this is more thought-provoking: if I had been the only person alive, my sins would have nailed him to the cross.

This is salvation. It can be summed up in the following four bible verses.

- God loves us.

  God "… desires all people to be saved and to come to the knowledge of the truth."1 Timothy 2:4.

- We sin.

  "for all have sinned and fall short of the glory of God," Romans 3:23.

- God responds.

  "For one will scarcely die for a righteous person—though perhaps for a good person - one would dare even to die but God shows his love for us in that while we were still sinners, Christ died for us." Romans 5:8-9.

- We must choose.

  "Because, if you confess with your mouth that Jesus is Lord and believe in your heart that God raised him from the dead, you will be saved. For with the heart one believes and is justified, and with the mouth one confesses and is saved." Romans 10: 9-10.

COPYRIGHT NOTICES

Tyndale House Publishers, Inc., Carol Stream, Illinois 60188.

BOOKS IN THE SERIES

Exploring the Gospel of Luke

If you found the section on How to Study the Bible helpful, especially the example from the Gospel of Luke on page 50, this book is for you.

It uses the same method described here. Each chapter includes a set of questions based on observation, interpretation and application steps, followed by opportunities for personal reflection.

Buy 'Exploring the Gospel of Luke One Chapter at a Time' from Amazon.